Who cares about Animal Rights?

illustrated by
Arlette Lavie

Child's Play (International) Ltd
Swindon   Bologna   New York
© 1992 M. Twinn   ISBN 0–85953–358–1   Printed in Singapore
Library of Congress Number 92-10852

Who loves animals?

We love our pets.

Some, like cats and dogs,
are our friends.
They play with us.
We enjoy their company.
We are sad, when they die.

In return, it is our duty
to take care of them.
Pets have rights to food, shelter
and exercise and to be kept clean.

Small, helpless and trusting,
baby animals make us feel tender.
We like to watch them grow.

We feel they have a right
to our care and protection.

Some animals share our lives,
our work and play.

We are grateful for
their special gifts,
their strength,
intelligence
and loyalty.

They do what we want,
and we have a duty
to look after them.

Do they still have a right to our loyalty
when they are no longer useful?

WILDLIFE RESERVE

To meet wild animals face to face,
close to where we live, is thrilling.

Shouldn't we keep
as many places as possible
where they can live naturally?

We learn from books and TV
about beautiful, strange
or fierce animals in far-away places.

Most of us never have a chance
to see them in the wild.
But would our world be poorer without them?

We have a right to protect
ourselves from dangerous animals.

But is there any need to harm them,
if we can just keep out of their way?

We don't love
all animals all the time.

Some animals are pests.
They eat our food
or spread disease
or damage our homes or crops.

So, we kill them.

Many pests are part of a chain.
Killing them may affect
numbers of animals they eat
or that eat them.

The methods we use to kill them
may harm other animals, too.
Or us. Especially if we use poisons.

Who decides which animals are pests
or what to do about them?

Some animals hunt others for food.
It is natural.
They have no choice.

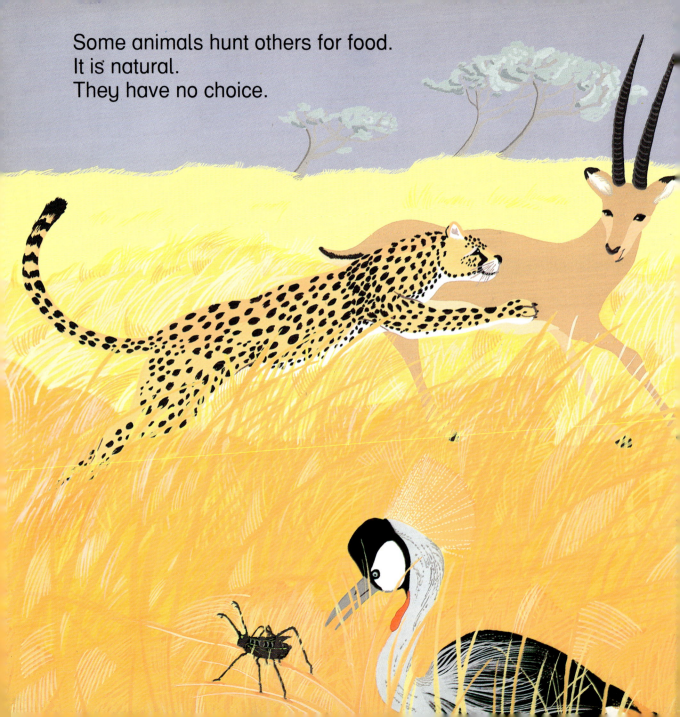

So, if humans eat meat,
surely, we have the right
to hunt and fish, too?

Are there limits?
Don't *we* have a choice?

We have been farmers for thousands of years.

We have learned to rear animals
in great numbers.

We kill them, for food, clothing,
and for other purposes,
often while they are young.

Don't we have the right?
Do we have any choice?

How many foods can you see?
How many come from animals?

What else can you see that
comes from animals?

Could we use anything else instead?

In zoos, we can see animals
we would never have a chance
to see in the wild.
Zoos, today, protect species
that human beings have endangered.

But some zoos are more fun for us than for the animals

If there have to be zoos, shouldn't they be places
where animals can live safe, healthy and active lives?

Is it right to keep wild animals in cages?

TIGER
PANTHERA TIGRIS

Many people enjoy hunting,
fishing and animal sports.

Hunters enjoy being close to nature,
the thrill of the chase, the kill.
They claim that it is their right.

Other people think it is barbarič
to *enjoy* hunting and fishing,
particularly, when there is no need
and there is so little wildlife left.

What do you think?

How much food does each of us need? How much meat?
Can people live healthily without meat?
Why do we waste so much food?

There are more and more people in the world
and it is the farmers' job to feed them.

People who breed, slaughter or transport animals sometimes forget to treat them kindly.

People who eat meat should be slow to criticize. But we should ask: is it right not to allow farm animals to move, eat or breed freely or to enjoy daylight?

Whether we eat meat or not, shouldn't we at least insist that farm animals are reared free from stress and killed without cruelty?

Most of us wear animal skins,
especially shoe leather.

How much fur or leather
do we really need?
Could we find alternatives?

Research helps doctors to save lives.

New methods, medicines
and cosmetics have to be tested.

But are painful experiments
on millions of animals necessary?

Animals feel pain like we do.
Surely, their distress matters?

What kind of people are we,
if we don't find alternatives
to cruel experiments
on animals?

We love our pets, but is it right
to buy and sell animals like objects,
to treat them like toys or to keep them in cages?
Many die on the journey from far-away places.

We decide where pets live, what they eat,
whether they may reproduce
and, often, when they shall die.

We may not have enough money
to feed our pets. We may be too lazy
or too frail to give them exercise.

People are often selfish or ignorant.
Some are deliberately cruel.

Most pets are well cared for.
But who benefits most? Pets or us?

Is the world big enough for us to share with other animals?

We always need more space, timber, stone, fuel, and water.
We destroy the natural environment to create homes,
hotels, factories, mines and farms.

Often, we are just careless.

Some people think the planet was made
for us, that taming nature is progress
and that animals exist to serve
our purposes. Do you agree?

The sort of world we are creating
is stressful to other animals and to us.
If we poison the planet
and disturb the balance of nature,
in the end, will we destroy ourselves?

We need space for wild animals and ourselves to roam free.
We must learn to treat all animals with respect.

We can't do much on our own. We can't change human nature.
Children can't do a lot. But we can all do something.

It is surprising how many parents are prepared to listen.
We can tell them what we want to eat.
We can say what we think about cruelty.
About hunting. About zoos. About production-line farming.

We can ask them what they think and why they let
other people make our decisions for us .

We can take care of our pets or choose not to have them.

We can decide now what we will do when we grow up.
It's our future.